KOSOVO TRAVE
2023-20

C000103272

Find the Rich Legacy and Regular Magnificence of Kosovo: Your comprehensive Travel Guide for the Place that is known for History and Appeal"

By

JOHN PETER

TABLE OF CONTENT

WELCOME

Step into a place where there is dazzling history, rich culture, and warm friendliness. As you adventure into this charming country, you will be submerged in the excellence of its different scenes and the flexibility of its kin.

The second you show up, you will be embraced by a feeling of having a place, as Kosovo's accommodating local people stretch out their open arms to welcome you. Here, customs and innovation mix flawlessly, offering you a one of a kind encounter like no other.

Investigate the antiquated legacy that reverberations through the old remnants and archeological destinations dispersed across the land. Thoroughly enjoy the appeal of curious towns where time appears to stop, and witness the building wonders that have endured everyday hardship.

Enjoy your faculties in the clamoring markets, where the fragrance of heavenly nearby treats floats through the air. Relish the divine kinds of customary food, similar to the scrumptious "flija" or the good "," while tasting on areas of strength for some, Turkish espresso.

Kosovo's regular magnificence will leave you entranced. Navigate through lofty mountains, wandering streams, and verdant valleys, offering incalculable open doors for experience searchers and nature sweethearts the same. Climb to stunning pinnacles, find stowed away cascades, or basically loosen up by the tranquil lakeshores.

The core of Kosovo lies in its kin, whose glow and versatility will move you. Find out about their accounts, their practices, and their excursion towards a more promising time to come. Witness the agreeable conjunction of various societies and religions, and embrace the soul of solidarity that ties the country together.

As the sun sets over Kosovo's viewpoint, get ready to be captivated by the energetic nightlife that wakes up in its urban areas. Participate in the vivacious music and dance, praising life and the soul of harmony.

Welcome to Kosovo, where the past interlaces with the present, and the commitment of a superior tomorrow sparkles splendidly. Embrace excellence, drench yourself in the way of life, and make recollections that will wait in your heart for eternity.

INTRODUCTION

Settled in the core of the Balkans, Kosovo is a place that is known for rich history, various cultures, and stunning scenes. This little, landlocked region is situated in Southeastern Europe, lining Serbia toward the north and east, Montenegro toward the northwest, Albania toward the southwest, and North Macedonia toward the southeast. Notwithstanding its moderately minimal size, Kosovo's importance on the worldwide stage is significant, as it has been a point of convergence of verifiable and international improvements for quite a long time. Kosovo's set of experiences is set apart by a mix of old civic establishments, with hints of Illyrians, Romans, Byzantines, and Ottomans leaving their permanent engravings on the locale. Notwithstanding, it was during the late twentieth century that Kosovo acquired global consideration because of the complex and in some cases violent situation that developed.

The late twentieth century saw the crumbling of the previous Communist Government Republic of Yugoslavia, prompting a progression of contentions and battles among its constituent republics. Kosovo turned into a milestone for ethnic strains between the Albanian greater part and the Serbian minority, finishing in an overwhelming outfitted struggle in the last part of the 1990s. The contention pulled in worldwide consideration and in the end prompted NATO's mediation in 1999, which finished the threats and laid out a global organization in Kosovo.

In February 2008, Kosovo proclaimed its freedom, which was perceived by countless nations all over the planet. In any case, Serbia, supported by its partners, wouldn't perceive Kosovo's power, bringing about continuous conciliatory and political difficulties.

Today, Kosovo is a youthful country that keeps on making progress toward strength, thriving, and incorporation into the global local area. The nation flaunts an energetic social legacy, displayed through its practices, expressions, and festivities. Guests to Kosovo can investigate antiquated forts, noteworthy landmarks, and pleasant scenes that mirror the country's well established past.

The number of inhabitants in Kosovo is overwhelmingly Albanian, with Albanian being the authority language. Its capital, Pristina, fills in as the social, political, and financial focus of the country. While Kosovo faces a few financial difficulties, its kin's flexibility and assurance to fabricate a splendid future are obvious, making it an enrapturing location for those trying to investigate a remarkable mix of history, culture, and regular magnificence.

In this prologue to Kosovo, we will set out on an excursion through its past, present, and expected future, revealing the quintessence of a country endeavoring to cut its way on the planet

ABOUT KOSOVO

Gotten comfortably to the center of the Balkans, Kosovo is a spot that is known for rich history, different culture, and staggering scenes. This little, landlocked district is arranged in Southeastern Europe, lining Serbia northward and east, Montenegro toward the northwest, Albania toward the southwest, and North Macedonia toward the southeast. Despite its modestly negligible size, Kosovo's significance on the overall stage is huge, as it has been a place of intermingling of obvious and global enhancements for a seriously prolonged stretch of time. Kosovo's arrangement of encounters is separate by a blend of old metro foundations, with traces of Illyrians, Romans, Byzantines, and Ottomans leaving their super durable etchings on the region. Regardless, it was during the late 20th century that Kosovo procured worldwide thought due to the mind boggling and now and again fierce circumstance that created.

The late 20th century saw the disintegrating of the past Socialist Government Republic of Yugoslavia, inciting a movement of disputes and fights among its constituent republics. Kosovo transformed into an achievement for ethnic strains between the Albanian larger part and the Serbian minority, competing in a mind-boggling equipped battle in the last piece of the 1990s. The conflict pulled in overall thought and in the end provoked NATO's intervention in 1999, which completed the dangers and spread out a worldwide association in Kosovo.

In February 2008, Kosovo announced its opportunity, which was seen by endless countries all around the planet. Regardless, Serbia, upheld by its accomplices, wouldn't see Kosovo's power, achieving consistent mollifying and political challenges.

Today, Kosovo is an energetic country that continues to gain ground toward strength, flourishing, and consolidation into the worldwide neighborhood. The country parades a vivacious social heritage, shown through its practices, articulations, and celebrations. Visitors to Kosovo can examine old-fashioned posts, imperative milestones, and wonderful scenes that reflect the nation's deep rooted past.

The quantity of occupants in Kosovo is predominantly Albanian, with Albanian being the power language. Its capital, Pristina, fills in as the social, political, and monetary focal point of the country. While Kosovo faces a couple of monetary troubles, its family's adaptability and confirmation to create an impressive future are self-evident, making it an enchanting area for those attempting to explore a noteworthy blend of history, culture, and customary greatness.

In this preface to Kosovo, we will set out on a trip through its past, present, and expected future, uncovering the pith of a nation trying to cut its direction in the world

GEOGRAPHY AND CLIMATE OF KOSOVO

Kosovo is a landlocked nation situated in the Balkans, in Southeastern Europe. It imparts lines to Serbia toward the north and east, North Macedonia toward the south, Albania toward the west, and Montenegro toward the northwest. The capital and biggest city of Kosovo is Pristina.

Topography of Kosovo:

Kosovo is described by a different scene that incorporates mountains, fields, and valleys. The focal locale is overwhelmed by the immense Dukagjini Valley, while the western piece of the nation is bumpy, with the Šar Mountains denoting the line with North Macedonia. The Rugova Mountains, a piece of the Prokletije range, lie in the northwestern locale of Kosovo, close to the line with Montenegro.

The country's two fundamental waterways are the White Drin (Drini I Bardhë) and the South Morava (Morava e Jugut). These streams assume a fundamental part in giving water assets to different motivations.

Environment of Kosovo:

Kosovo encounters a mainland environment, portrayed by cool winters and blistering summers. In any case, because of the assorted geography, there can be some variety in the environment across various areas of the country.

Winter: Winters in Kosovo, especially in the hilly regions, are cold and frequently joined by snowfall. Temperatures can decrease beneath freezing, and rugged areas might encounter weighty snowfall throughout the cold weather months.

Spring: Spring is a momentary season when the weather conditions slowly become milder. The mountains begin to shed their snow, and the scenes become greener as the vegetation blossoms.

Summer: Summers in Kosovo are by and large warm and dry, with temperatures frequently arriving at above 30°C (86°F) during the day. The fields and valleys can turn out to be very warm, however the hilly districts offer a more lovely environment, making them well known objections for the summer travel industry.

Autumn: Harvest time is one more momentary season, set apart by cooler temperatures and beautiful foliage as the trees get ready for winter.

In general, Kosovo's environment is affected by its landlocked position and the encompassing geological elements, which can prompt temperature limits and varieties between various pieces of the country. It's crucial for note that environment examples can change after some time, so it's prudent to allude to later and limited hotspots for the most modern data on Kosovo's geology and environment

BRIEF HISTORY OF KOSOVO

Kosovo, situated in the Balkans, has a long and complex history molded by different developments and clashes. Here is a concise outline:

Old and Bygone eras: The area that is currently Kosovo has been occupied since antiquated times, with proof of human settlement tracing all the way back to the Paleolithic period. Since the beginning of time, it was essential for different domains and realms, including the Roman Domain, Byzantine Domain, and Serbian middle age states.

Ottoman Rule: In the late fourteenth 100 years, the Ottoman Realm vanquished the locale, and Kosovo stayed under Ottoman rule for about five centuries. During this period, the populace saw a blend of societies, religions, and dialects, adding to the ethnic variety that portrays Kosovo today.

Public Arousing and Autonomy: By the late nineteenth and mid twentieth hundreds of years, the possibility of patriotism and freedom spread all through the Balkans. The Albanian populace in Kosovo started supporting their public privileges and independence. The district's status was a subject of dispute between the Ottoman Domain, Serbia, and other Balkan states.

Interwar Period and Universal Conflicts: After the Balkan Wars and WWI, Kosovo turned out to be essential for the Realm of Serbs, Croats, and Slovenes (later known as Yugoslavia). Under Yugoslavian rule, Kosovo was an independent district with a huge Albanian larger part. In any case, strains between ethnic Albanians and Serbs endured.

Tito's Yugoslavia: After The Second Great War, Josip Broz Tito laid out a communist government republic known as Yugoslavia, containing six republics, including Serbia and the independent region of Kosovo. During Tito's standard, Kosovo's independence was extended, and Albanians stood firm on key footings in the territorial government.

The 1980s and the Ascent of Patriotism: In the last part of the 1980s, under the administration of Slobodan Milošević, Serbian patriotism flooded, prompting the repudiation of Kosovo's independence in 1989. The Serbian government assumed command over the district, prompting expanded constraint and oppression of the Albanian populace.

Kosovo Battle: In the last part of the 1990s, pressures arose, and an equipped struggle emitted between Serbian powers and the Kosovo Freedom Armed force (KLA), looking for autonomy for Kosovo. The conflict brought about huge losses and broad denials of basic liberties.

NATO Mediation and Freedom: In 1999, NATO interceded militarily, directing airstrikes against Serbian powers, which eventually prompted the withdrawal of Serbian soldiers from Kosovo. The Unified Countries then, at that point, directed the locale until 2008 when Kosovo pronounced freedom. Starting around my last update in September 2021, north of 100 nations have perceived Kosovo as a free state, however Serbia actually thinks of it as a feature of its domain.

Kosovo's way to dependability and improvement has been trying since autonomy, with issues connected with administration, between ethnic relations, financial advancement actually requiring consideration. The locale stays a subject of international interest, with continuous endeavors by the global local area to encourage enduring harmony and steadiness.

CHAPTER ONE

Best Time To Visit Kosovo

The best chance to visit Kosovo relies upon your inclinations for climate, exercises, and groups. Kosovo encounters a mainland environment with four unmistakable seasons. Here are the various seasons to consider:

Spring (April to June): Spring is a lovely chance to visit Kosovo as the scene wakes up with blossoming blossoms and rich plant life. The weather conditions are gentle and lovely, with temperatures going from 15°C to 25°C (59°F to 77°F). It's an optimal time for outside exercises, investigating authentic locales, and partaking in the normal magnificence of the country.

Summer (July to August): Summer can get very sweltering in Kosovo, with temperatures frequently surpassing 30°C (86°F) during the day. In the event that you appreciate the warm climate and wouldn't fret the intensity, this is an extraordinary opportunity to visit. Summer is additionally the pinnacle vacationer season, so well known attractions and places of interest might be packed. Consider visiting toward the beginning of July or late August to keep away from the pinnacle swarms.

Harvest time (September to October): Pre-winter is one more wonderful chance to visit Kosovo. The weather conditions are as yet lovely, with temperatures going from 15°C to 20°C (59°F to 68°F). The foliage begins evolving colors, making pleasant scenes. It's an incredible time for touring, climbing, and getting a charge out of nearby celebrations and comprehensive developments.

Winter (November to February): Winter in Kosovo is cold, with temperatures frequently dipping under freezing. On the off chance that you appreciate winter sports like skiing and snowboarding, this is the best opportunity to visit the nation's ski resorts, like Brezovica. In any case, remember that bumpy regions may be blocked off because of weighty snowfall.

All in all, the best opportunity to visit Kosovo generally relies upon your inclinations and inclinations. Spring and fall offer agreeable climate and wonderful landscape, while summer is dynamic with exercises however can be packed. Winter is great for winter sports aficionados. Consider your ideal encounters and plan likewise for a significant excursion to Kosovo.

Entering Requirements to Kosovo

This is to furnish you with a general direction on entering Kosovo. If it's not too much trouble, note that the movement prerequisites could have changed from that point forward, so it's fundamental to check the most exceptional data from true government sources or important specialists prior to arranging your outing.

Entering Kosovo generally includes thinking about visa necessities, identification legitimacy, and any Coronavirus related conventions. Here is a general framework of the run of the mill necessities:

Passport: Guarantee that your identification is legitimate for somewhere around a half year past your arranged date of takeoff from Kosovo. A few nations may likewise require a particular number of clear pages for visa stamps.

Visa: Contingent upon your ethnicity, you might have to get a visa prior to heading out to Kosovo. Check with the closest Kosovo international safe haven or department to check whether you want a visa and what kind of visa would be suitable for your motivation of movement (e.g., vacationer, business, work, and so on.).

Coronavirus Limitations: Because of the continuous Coronavirus pandemic, there may be explicit section necessities connected with testing, quarantine, or inoculation. Actually take a look at the most recent updates from the authority Kosovo government site or the international safe haven/office for any

Coronavirus related conventions that you want to follow.

Travel Protection: Fitting to have travel protection covers clinical costs and crisis bringing home while you're in Kosovo.

Greeting Letter (if relevant): Contingent upon your justification for visiting Kosovo (e.g., business, family visit), you could require a greeting letter from a host in Kosovo expressing the reason and span of your visit.

Verification of Adequate Assets: Movement authorities might request proof that you have sufficient cash to cover your costs during your visit in Kosovo, like bank proclamations or a letter from your manager.

Bring Ticket back: It's generally expected to have a return or forward pass to show that you intend to leave Kosovo after your visit.

If it's not too much trouble, recall that these prerequisites can change contingent upon your ethnicity and the reason for your visit. It's crucial for twofold check with true sources prior to making any movement plans to Kosovo

Getting there

1. **Air Travel**:

The most straightforward method for arriving at Kosovo is via air. The country's super worldwide air terminal is the Pristina Global Air terminal (PRN). A few carriers offer trips to Pristina from different urban communities in Europe and then some. A few significant carriers that have worked trips to Pristina incorporate Turkish Carriers, Lufthansa, Air Serbia, and Wizz Air. Notwithstanding, it's fundamental to check the ongoing flight choices and timetables nearer to your takeoff date.

2. **Land Travel:**

Kosovo is open via land from adjoining nations, and there are a few line intersections. The principal section focuses are from Serbia, North Macedonia, Albania, and Montenegro. Transport administrations and confidential cabs are accessible for land travel, making it generally simple to move around the locale.

3. **Transport Travel**:

Transports are a well known method of transportation for both homegrown and worldwide travel inside the Balkans. There are regular transport associations with Kosovo from significant urban communities in the adjoining nations. The transports are for the most part reasonable and actually agreeable.

4. **Train Travel**:

Kosovo doesn't have a broad rail route organization, and there are no immediate global train administrations to the country. Nonetheless, you can arrive at adjoining nations via train and afterward proceed with your excursion to Kosovo through transports or other ground transportation.

5. **Vehicle Rental:**

Leasing a vehicle can be a possibility for voyagers who lean toward greater adaptability and freedom in investigating the country. A few vehicle rental organizations work in Pristina and other significant urban communities in Kosovo. In any case, know that driving circumstances and street framework might change, so practice wariness and actually take a look at neighborhood traffic guidelines.

6. **Neighborhood Transportation**:

Inside Kosovo, you can utilize transports, taxicabs, or offer cabs (called "furgons") to get around urban communities and towns. Taxis are generally accessible in Pristina and other metropolitan places. Furgons are a well known method of transport for brief distances among towns and towns.

7. **Visa Necessities**:

Prior to heading out to Kosovo, checking the visa necessities for your nationality is fundamental. Kosovo singularly pronounced freedom in 2008, however its status remains a subject of global acknowledgment. Starting around 2021, Kosovo was not an individual from the European Association, so EU visa strategies probably won't have any significant bearing.

As movement guidelines, flight choices, and other transportation subtleties could change over the long run, I suggest checking with true government sites, aircrafts, and legitimate travel services nearer to your movement date for the latest data on transportation to Kosovo.

Accomodations in Kosovo

Kosovo, a landlocked country in the Balkans, is known for its rich history, energetic culture, and delightful scenes. The capital city, PRI¡Tina, and other significant urban communities offer a scope of facilities to suit various inclinations and spending plans. Hotels: In metropolitan regions like PriÅ¡tina, Prizren, and Gjakova, you can find various lodgings going from extravagant properties to more spending plan cordial choices. Worldwide lodging networks and nearby store inns take care of various kinds of explorers.

Guesthouses and Inns: For spending plan explorers or those looking for a more neighborhood experience, guesthouses and lodgings are accessible in different urban communities. These spots frequently give a more cozy and social environment, making them ideal for meeting different voyagers.

Lofts and Excursion Rentals: In bigger urban areas, you can find lofts or get-away rentals presented through stages like Airbnb. These choices can be perfect in the event that you favor a more home-like insight during your visit.

Provincial Facilities: On the off chance that you intend to investigate the open country or more modest towns, you could go over family-run guesthouses or customary homestays. These can offer an extraordinary chance to drench yourself in neighborhood culture.

Internet Booking: Numerous convenience choices in Kosovo can be reserved web-based through famous travel sites and stages. Prior to your excursion, consider utilizing these stages to tie down your favored spot to remain.

As you plan your excursion to Kosovo, remember that the nation has been constantly further developing its travel industry framework, and new facilities could have opened up since my last update. Furthermore, consistently survey late voyager audits and evaluations to get a superior comprehension of the quality and administrations given by various facilities.

Ultimately, it's really smart to get to know nearby traditions and culture to guarantee a conscious and pleasant stay in Kosovo. Partake in your excursion to this delightful Balkan country!

Things To Pack For Kosovo Visit

While pressing for a little while to Kosovo, it's fundamental to consider the season and the exercises you intend to participate in. Here is a general pressing rundown to kick you off:

Travel Archives:

Identification (substantial for no less than a half year)

Visa (whenever required, really look at the ongoing visa necessities)

Travel progarchives Agenda

Agenda and convenience subtleties

Clothing:

Lightweight, breathable attire for summer (May to September)

Hotter layers for spring and harvest time (April, October)

Winter clothing (November to Spring) if visiting during the colder months

Rainproof coat or umbrella

Open to strolling shoes or tennis shoes

Dressier outfit for formal events (if appropriate)

Bathing suit (for lodging pools or underground aquifers, if significant)

Wellbeing and Individual Consideration:

Professionally prescribed drugs (whenever required)

Essential medical aid unit (bandages, pain killers, germ-free cream)

Individual cleanliness items (toothbrush, toothpaste, cleanser, and so on.)

Sunscreen and lip salve with SPF

Bug repellent

Hand sanitizer and moist disposable clothes

Hardware:

Travel connector and converter (assuming that different fitting sorts and voltage)
Cell phone and charger
Camera or camcorder with extras
Power bank for charging in a hurry
Cash and Assets:
Neighborhood cash (Kosovo utilizes the Euro)
Credit/charge cards
Travel wallet or cash belt
Keep a duplicate of significant reports like your visa and travel protection independently.
Miscellaneous:
Daypack or backpack for road trips
Water bottle (to remain hydrated)
Pocket-sized manual or guide
Travel pad and eye cover for long excursions
Language phrasebook or language interpretation application (Albanian and Serbian are the principal dialects spoken)
Amusement (book, tablet, or music player)
Snacks for the excursion
Aware Clothing:

Assuming you intend to visit strict locales, bring unobtrusive apparel that covers your shoulders and knees.

Make sure to pack as per the particular season and exercises you have arranged. Kosovo has lovely scenes and a rich history, so be ready to investigate and partake in your visit!

CHAPTER TWO

Understand Kosovo

Kosovo is a little landlocked locale situated in the Balkans, in southeastern Europe. It holds authentic importance and has been at the focal point of different political and social turns of events. To comprehend Kosovo, we want to dig into its set of experiences, geology, culture, and political circumstance **Authenticity Foundation**:

Kosovo's set of experiences is rich and complicated, molded by different human advancements and realms throughout the long term. In old times, the locale was possessed by Illyrian clans. Afterward, it fell under Roman, Byzantine, and Ottoman rule. During the fourteenth and fifteenth hundreds of years, Kosovo turned into the heartland of the archaic Serbian state, known for the unbelievable Skirmish of Kosovo Polje in 1389, where Serbian powers battled against the Ottoman Realm.

The Ottoman Time and Ethnic Variety:

In the late fourteenth hundred years, the Ottoman Domain vanquished Kosovo, and it stayed under Ottoman rule for very nearly five centuries until the twentieth 100 years. During this time, the area experienced critical segment changes, and its populace turned out to be all the more ethnically different, including Albanians, Serbs, and different gatherings.

The Ascent of Patriotism and **Struggle**:

The nineteenth and twentieth hundreds of years saw the ascent of patriotism across the Balkans, including Kosovo. Public character turned into a huge variable, prompting pressures between the

Albanian and Serbian people group. The circumstance deteriorated after the breakdown of the Ottoman Realm, as the two Albanians and Serbs guaranteed verifiable and social freedoms to the land.

Kosovo's Independence and War:

In 1945, after The Second Great War, Kosovo turned into an independent region inside the Communist Government Republic of Yugoslavia, driven by Josip Broz Tito. Nonetheless, pressures between the Serbian minority and the Albanian greater part kept on stewing. In the last part of the 1980s, Serbian pioneer Slobodan Milošević repudiated Kosovo's independence, igniting a progression of fights and requests for freedom by the Albanian populace.

Kosovo War and Autonomy:

In the last part of the 1990s, the circumstance swelled into a full-scale furnished struggle known as the Kosovo War. The conflict included ethnic purging and outrages executed by Serbian powers against the Albanian populace, inciting global mediation. In 1999, NATO sent off a tactical mission against Yugoslavia, which prompted the withdrawal of Serbian powers and the foundation of the Unified Countries Break Organization Mission in Kosovo (UNMIK). Kosovo declared its autonomy from Serbia on February 17, 2008.

Global Acknowledgment and **Political Circumstance**:

The statement of freedom has been a subject of debate. Starting around my last update in September 2021, Kosovo's freedom has been perceived by more than 100 nations, including the US and most European Association countries. Be that as it may, Serbia, upheld by Russia, won't perceive Kosovo as a sovereign state.

Current Circumstance:

Kosovo's way to state-building and strength has been tested. Issues like ethnic pressures, defilement, and financial battles keep on presenting deterrents to its turn of events. Worldwide help and political endeavors are progressing to address these difficulties and cultivate a supportable and serene future for the district.

By and large, understanding Kosovo requires thinking about its authentic setting, ethnic variety, complex political circumstance, and the endeavors of the worldwide local area to encourage dependability and improvement. Similarly as with any locale with a turbulent past, it's urgent to move toward conversations about Kosovo with responsiveness and a consciousness of the different points of view held by various networks and countries.

PEOPLE AND CULTURE OF KOSOVO

Ethnic Arrangement: Kosovo's populace is dominantly composed of two significant ethnic gatherings: Albanians and Serbs. Albanians structure the greater part, representing around 90% of the populace, while Serbs make up a huge minority. Other than Albanians and Serbs, there are more modest networks of Bosniaks, Turks, Roma, Ashkali, and Egyptians, among others.

Albanian Impact: The Albanian culture assumes a prevailing part in Kosovo, essentially because of the larger part ethnic gathering. The Albanian language is the authority language of the nation, and it unmistakably affects neighborhood customs, customs, and lifestyle.

Religion: Most of Kosovo's populace rehearses Islam, with Sunni Islam being the most common branch. There is likewise a Christian minority, including both Customary Christianity (rehearsed predominantly by Serbs) and Catholicism.

History and Personality: Kosovo has an intricate history, frequently set apart by political and ethnic pressures. The area holds huge authentic and social significance for the two Serbs and Albanians, adding to the assorted characters of its kin.

Cuisine: Kosovo's cooking mirrors the impact of both Mediterranean and Balkan culinary customs. Well known dishes incorporate "flija" (a layered pie), "qebapa" (barbecued minced meat wieners), and different customary dairy items.

Customary Music and Dance: Music and dance are vital to Kosovo's social articulation. Conventional music frequently incorporates a blend of society, traditional, and metropolitan impacts. The "valle" is a well known conventional dance, performed during festivities and merriments.

Family and Social Design: The idea of family and broadened connection holds huge significance in Kosovo's way of life. Family ties areas of strength for are, get-togethers and shared occasions assume a fundamental part in individuals' lives.

Handicrafts: Kosovo has a rich practice of crafted works, including many-sided weaving, floor covering winding around, and ceramics. These specialties exhibit the abilities and innovativeness of neighborhood craftsmans and are in many cases gone down through ages.

Celebrations and Festivities: Kosovo celebrates different social and strict celebrations, like Eid al-Fitr (denoting the finish of Ramadan), Bajrami (Albanian name for Eid), and Universal Christmas. The Freedom Day of Kosovo, on February seventeenth, is likewise a huge public festival.

Contemporary Difficulties: Regardless of its energetic social legacy, Kosovo has confronted difficulties connected with ethnic pressures, financial turn of events, and political solidness. The nation has been making progress toward building a brought together personality while regarding its multicultural nature.

It's critical to take note that societies are dynamic and advance over the long haul. Accordingly, the data introduced here may not completely address the present status of Kosovo's kin and culture. To acquire a more state-of-the-art understanding, I prescribe alluding to late sources and drawing in with current news and writing regarding the matter.

ART AND ARCHITECTURE OF KOSOVO

Craftsmanship in Kosovo:
Conventional Society Workmanship: Kosovo has major areas of strength for any kind of craftsmanship, including winding around, weaving, earthenware, and woodcarving. These specialties are in many cases gone down through ages and are esteemed for their multifaceted plans and dynamic tones.

Iconography: Kosovo has a long history of strict craftsmanship, especially as strict symbols. The Serbian Customary Church has been instrumental in safeguarding and advancing this artistic expression. Numerous strict symbols can be tracked down in cloisters and chapels all through the district.

Contemporary Craftsmanship: as of late, contemporary workmanship has been thriving in Kosovo. The capital city, Pristina, is home to a few craftsmanship displays and social focuses that exhibit crafted by neighborhood and global specialists. Kosovo's contemporary workmanship scene is assorted, mirroring the country's tempestuous past and its ongoing desires.

Design in Kosovo:

Archaic Engineering: Kosovo flaunts a few very much protected middle age compositional wonders. Striking models incorporate the Gračanica Cloister, an UNESCO World Legacy Site, known for its remarkable Byzantine design and dazzling frescoes. The Dečani Cloister is another significant site, highlighting a blend of Byzantine, Romanesque, and Gothic components.

Ottoman Impact: Kosovo's design likewise grandstands the impact of the Ottoman Realm, which governed the district for quite a long time. Ottoman design is clear in the various mosques, hammams (Turkish showers), and marketplaces dispersed the nation over. The Sinan Pasha Mosque in Prizren and the Majestic Mosque in Peja are two phenomenal instances of Ottoman-style mosques in Kosovo.

Current Engineering: In metropolitan habitats like Pristina, present day design should be visible in government structures, business buildings, and neighborhoods. While a few contemporary structures draw motivation from conventional styles, others show pioneer and functionalist plans.

Strict Variety: Kosovo is home to a blend of strict structures, mirroring its different populace. Other than the Serbian Universal cloisters and Ottoman-time mosques, there are additionally Roman Catholic holy places and different other strict designs.

Throughout the long term, Kosovo has confronted huge difficulties, including clashes and political shakiness. Notwithstanding these hardships, its specialty and design have persevered as a significant part of the nation's personality and social legacy. It's actually significant that there might have been further turns of events and changes in the craftsmanship and engineering of Kosovo.

Environment Of Kosovo

Kosovo is a district situated in the Balkans, in Southeastern Europe. It declared freedom from Serbia in 2008, yet its sway remains a subject of worldwide discussion, as not all nations perceive its autonomy. Kosovo is a landlocked nation lined by Serbia toward the north and east, North Macedonia toward the south, Albania toward the west, and Montenegro toward the northwest.

Climate and Geology:

Kosovo flaunts a different scene described by mountains, valleys, and fields TheeSharersr Mountains rule the southern district, while the Prokletije Mountains are in the west. The nation is important for the Dinaric Alps and the Balkan Landmass, adding to its rich regular magnificence. A few streams, including the Sitnica, Ibar, and Drini, course through the locale, giving water assets to different motivations.

Environment:

Kosovo encounters a mainland environment, with cold winters and warm summers. The environment is affected by its landlocked position and uneven landscape. Winters can be very unforgiving, with snowfall and low temperatures, while summers can be blistering and dry.

Biodiversity:

Kosovo's biodiversity is moderately assorted, taking into account its size and topographical elements. The nation is home to different plant and creature species, including oak, beech, and pine backwoods. Natural life incorporates species like earthy colored bears, wolves, wild hogs, foxes, and different bird species. Nonetheless, in the same way as other districts, Kosovo faces difficulties connected with natural surroundings obliteration and loss of biodiversity because of human exercises and urbanization.

Ecological Difficulties:

Kosovo, in the same way as other different nations, faces ecological difficulties that require consideration and activity. A portion of the central points of interest include:

Air and Water Contamination: Modern exercises and the consuming of petroleum derivatives add to air contamination, prompting medical issues and natural debasement. Also, ill-advised squandering the executives and horticultural practices can contaminate water sources.

Deforestation: Uncontrolled logging and land-use changes have prompted deforestation in specific regions, affecting biological systems and biodiversity.

Squander The executives: Kosovo faces difficulties in dealing with its waste successfully, prompting issues of littering and lacking removal, influencing both metropolitan and country regions.

Energy Reliance: The nation intensely depends on coal for its energy needs, prompting ozone depleting substance emanations and natural worries connected with environmental change.

Water The board: Water shortage and the executives stay big worries, especially during dry periods and because of obsolete framework.

Preservation Endeavors:

Endeavors are being made by the public authority, NGOs, and worldwide associations to address these natural difficulties and advance maintainability. Drives incorporate bringing issues to light about ecological issues, executing better waste administration works on, empowering sustainable power tasks, and supporting preservation endeavors for safeguarded regions.

Kindly note what is happening might have developed since my last update, and I suggest counseling later hotspots for the most cutting-edge data on the climate of Kosovo.

Festivals and Celebration in Kosovo

Kosovo had a few celebrations and festivities that held social, verifiable, and strict importance. Please keep in mind that new occurrences or modifications may have taken place. The following are some notable Kosovo festivals and celebrations:

Day of Independence Datata and Pavarsis): Independence Day, observed on February 17th, honors Kosovo's declaration of independence from Serbia in 2008. This significant national holiday is marked by numerous celebrations and events all over the country.

Day of the New Year (Viti i Ri): The first day of the new year is celebrated with a variety of parties, celebrations, and fireworks, just like it is in many other nations.

Bajrami i Vogl, or Eid al-Fitr, is A significant Islamic celebration denoting the finish of Ramadan, the long stretch of fasting. Prayers, feasting, and charitable acts are part of the celebration. The Islamic lunar calendar determines the annual date of Eid al-Fitr.

Bajrami i Madh, or Eid al-Adha, Another significant Islamic festival is Eid al-Adha, which is also known as the Feast of Sacrifice. It honors Ibrahim (Abraham)'s willingness to sacrifice his son in response to God's command. The date of Eid al-Adha additionally changes every year based on the Islamic lunar schedule.

Nowruz: Celebrated on the vernal equinox (around Spring 21st), Nowruz denotes the Persian New Year and is praised in many pieces of the Balkans, including Kosovo. Traditional music, dancing, and feasting make this a joyful time.

Day of the Gjakova (Dita e Gjakovs): Gjakova Day is a celebration of the culture and history of the city of Gjakova that takes place on April 25. It incorporates different far-reaching developments, exhibitions, and exercises.

Prishtina Day (Dita e Prishtinës): Prishtina Day, which is observed on May 1st, is dedicated to Prishtina, the capital city of Kosovo. The city's culture and accomplishments are celebrated through activities, concerts, and events.

Dokufest: Dokufest, an annual international documentary and short film festival in Prizren, is one of Kosovo's most prominent cultural events. Filmmakers and cinephiles from all over the world gather to exhibit their work and celebrate documentary filmmaking as a form of art.

Wine Celebrations: The wine industry in Kosovo is expanding, and numerous wine festivals are held throughout the year in various parts of the country. Visitors can sample a variety of wines at these celebrations of the local winemaking traditions.

These are just a few of the festivals and celebrations that took place in Kosovo up until the time of my most recent update. Recall that occasions and festivities could have developed or changed from that point forward, so it's dependably smart to check with refreshed sources to get the most recent data.

CHAPTER THREE

Top Attractions Of Kosovo

In the Balkans, Kosovo is known for its stunning natural landscapes, rich history, and cultural heritage. Here are a portion of the top attractions in Kosovo:

Monastery of Graanica: A masterpiece of architecture, this Serbian Orthodox monastery from the 14th century is listed as a UNESCO World Heritage Site. It is known for its stunning frescoes and represents the religious and cultural heritage of the nation.

Pristina: Kosovo's capital city, Pristina, offers a mix of verifiable tourist spots and present day attractions. The Imperial Mosque and the Newborn Monument, both of which are memorials to the nation's independence, must be visited.

Gjakova: a charming town known for its bustling bazaar and architecture in the Ottoman style. One of the largest Old Bazaars in the

Balkans, Gjakova's Old Bazaar is a lively place to learn about local culture.

Prizren: Prizren is a well-preserved Ottoman old town with cobbled streets, historic mosques, and the imposing Kalaja Fortress, which offers panoramic views of the city. It is frequently regarded as one of the most beautiful cities in Kosovo.

Region of Rugova: a natural wonder with its rugged mountains, deep canyons, and clear rivers that take your breath away. In the winter, the Rugova Valley offers activities like skiing, rock climbing, and hiking, making it ideal for outdoor enthusiasts.

Monastery of Decani: The Decani Monastery, another UNESCO World Heritage Site, is renowned for its remarkable frescoes and exquisite medieval architecture.

Mirusha Cascades: Mirusha Waterfalls, which are close to the town of Klina and offer a tranquil and picturesque natural setting, are a great spot for nature enthusiasts and photographers.

Bear Habitat: The Bear Sanctuary in Mramor provides a natural and secure environment for rescued bears that were previously kept in captivity.

Museum of Ethnology (Muzeu Etnologjik): This museum, which is in the town of Prizren, provides insights into the traditional culture and history of Kosovo.

Germia Field: Germia Park, which is close to Pristina and has swimming pools, sports fields, and hiking trails, is a popular destination for locals and tourists alike.

Please keep in mind that the situation and the options for tourists may have changed since my last update. Before making plans to visit Kosovo, it's always a good idea to check for the most recent information. Thanks for coming!

Outdoor Activities In Kosovo

Kosovo is a wonderful country with different scenes, offering a scope of outside exercises for nature sweethearts and experienced searchers. Here are a few open air exercises you can appreciate in Kosovo:

Climbing: Kosovo is speckled with various climbing trails, taking special care of all ability levels. The Detestable Mountains (Bjeshkët e Nemuna) in the western piece of the nation give shocking perspectives and testing journeys. Climb to the pinnacle of Gjeravica, the most noteworthy mountain in Kosovo, or investigate the Rugova Gully for a critical encounter.

Setting up camp: With its perfect nature and pleasant scenes, Kosovo offers incredible setting up camp open doors. Whether you decide to camp close to lakes, streams, or in the mountains, going through a night under the stars is a mind boggling method for interfacing with nature.

Rock Climbing: Rugova Gully is a well known objective for rock climbers. The tough precipices and staggering ravines give a novel climbing experience to the two fledglings and experienced climbers.

Skiing and Snowboarding: Throughout the cold weather months, make a beeline for Brezovica Ski Resort in the Shar Mountains for skiing and snowboarding. The retreat offers all around kept up with slants and stunning winter landscape.

Paragliding: Experience the excitement of flying over Kosovo's dazzling scenes by going paragliding. Areas like Gjilan and Pristina offer paragliding open doors with experienced teachers.

Boating and Kayaking: The Drini and Erenik waterways are incredible spots for whitewater boating and kayaking. Partake in the adrenaline rush as you explore through the rapids encompassed by gorgeous views.

Cycling: Get your bicycle and investigate the field of Kosovo. There are different cycling courses taking special care of various degrees of trouble. The cycling way from Pristina to Gračanica is a famous decision.

Birdwatching: Kosovo is home to an assortment of bird animal groups, making it a heaven for birdwatchers. The wetlands close to Lake

Badovc and Lake Radoniqi offer superb open doors for birdwatching.

Picnicking: Partake in a loosening up day with loved ones by having a cookout in one of the many stops or green regions dispersed all through the country. Germia Park in Pristina is a well known decision for picnics.

Visiting Public Parks: Investigate the public parks of Kosovo, like Sharri Public Park and Bjeshkët e Nemuna Public Park, where you can submerge yourself in the dazzling normal magnificence of the country.

Make sure to constantly observe security rules and guidelines while participating in outside exercises, and be aware of the climate to assist with protecting Kosovo's regular fortunes for people in the future to appreciate.

Nature Tour Of Kosovo

Welcome to the normal marvels of Kosovo! This stunning Balkan nation is home to a wide range of landscapes and abundant biodiversity. We should set out on a virtual nature visit to investigate a portion of its most stunning normal attractions:

Rugova Canyon: The stunning Gorge is where we begin our journey in the western part of Kosovo. This 25-kilometer-long canyon, formed by the Rugova River and surrounded by towering limestone cliffs, is a popular camping, hiking, and rock climbing destination. The flawless nature, outside air, and peaceful climate offer an ideal getaway from the hurrying around of day to day existence.

Sharri Public Park: We arrive at Sharri National Park, one of Kosovo's five national parks, as we move south. This protected area is a haven for nature lovers and spans the Ar Mountains. Various species of plants and animals can be found in the park, including dense forests of beech, pine, and spruce as well as wild animals like lynxes, wolves, and brown bears. The meadows are covered in vibrant wildflowers in the spring, providing a picturesque setting.

The Mirusha Falls: The stunning Mirusha Waterfalls, which are close to the town of Klina, are our next destination. A true gem of Kosovo, these cascading waterfalls are hard to find. The river has formed a series of waterfalls, which are awe-inspiring as the water cascades over the rocks to form natural pools that are ideal for a cool swim in the summer.

Park of the Sharr Mountains: How about we head toward the eastern piece of Kosovo, where the Sharr Mountains Public Park is standing by. The majestic Sharr Mountain range, which stretches across Albania, North Macedonia, and Kosovo, is the inspiration for the name of this park. Glacier lakes, alpine meadows, and dramatic peaks make up the region. The park is a great place to hike and look for wildlife.

Brezovica Ski Resort: For those who enjoy snow sports, Brezovica Ski Resort is a must-visit destination during the winter months. This resort, which is located in the Sharr Mountains, has slopes that are suitable for skiers and snowboarders of all levels. Brezovica is a beautiful place to hike and take in the stunning views of the surrounding mountains even in the summer.

Marble Cave of Gadime: The Gadime Marble Cave, which is near the town of Lipjan, comes into view as we return to the west. Stalagmites and stalactites from millions of years ago can be seen in this underground wonder's labyrinth of well-lit galleries and tunnels.

Gazivoda Lake: Our last objective is Lake Gazivoda, the biggest lake in Kosovo, arranged close to the northern line with Serbia. There are numerous opportunities to fish, boat, and unwind by the water's edge at this reservoir, as well as picturesque views.

You will be mesmerized by Kosovo's unspoiled beauty, diverse landscapes, and welcoming people during this nature tour. Therefore, whether you're looking for adventure or just peace and quiet, Kosovo has something for everyone who enjoys nature.

Setting Budget To Kosovo

When compared to many other European nations, Kosovo is generally regarded as an affordable destination.

For a good guess:

Accommodation: Hotels can range in price from €50 to €100 per night, while budget accommodations can range from €20 to €50 per night.

Food: A meal at a local restaurant may cost between €5 and €15, while street food and other less expensive options may be even more affordable.

Transportation: Public transportation is sensibly valued, and taxis are likewise moderately reasonable.

Activities and sights to see: Museum and attraction admission prices can vary, but they are typically affordable.

Miscellaneous: It's a good idea to have extra money on hand for last-minute purchases or souvenirs.

In general, a traveler on a budget may require between €40 and €60 per day, while a traveler on a budget may require between €70 and €100 per day. Notwithstanding, these are simply good guesses, and genuine costs will differ contingent upon your decisions and inclinations.

Consider researching the most recent prices and making adjustments based on your travel plans for a more precise budget.

Saving Money In Kosovo

Make a Spending plan: Begin by keeping track of your spending and income. Make a list of all of your regular expenses, including rent, utilities, food, transportation, and so on. This will provide you with a reasonable picture of where your cash is going and where you can scale back.

Reduce Unnecessary Costs: Examine your spending patterns to find areas where you can save money. For instance, attempt to restrict eating out, diversion costs, and motivation buys.

Instead of purchasing coffee frocafÃ©cafe, think about making your own.

Examine Costs: Compare prices from a variety of merchants or stores prior to making significant purchases. Take advantage of promotions, discounts, and sales.

Save money on utilities: Be aware of how much energy you use. Switch out lights, machines, and hardware when not being used. If you want to save money on electricity, think about using appliances and light bulbs that use less energy.

Transportation: To save money on fuel and upkeep, whenever possible, take public transportation or carpool. Consider selling your car and using other means of transportation instead if you rarely use it.

Home Cooked Food: It can be expensive to eat out, so try to prepare meals at home. To prevent food waste, plan your meals in advance and purchase groceries accordingly.

Make a fund for an emergency: Start making an emergency fund out of a portion of your income. When unexpected expenses occur, having a financial safety net will keep you from going into debt.

Stop using credit cards: Visas can be advantageous, yet they can likewise prompt obligation in the event that is not utilized mindfully. Instead of using credit, try paying for your purchases with cash or debit cards.

Don't make rash purchases: Prior to purchasing something, get some margin to believe in the event that it's a vital buy or on the other hand on the off chance that it's something you can manage without. Avoid buying things on the spot, especially if they are expensive.

Reduce Bank Fees: Search for banks or monetary foundations that propose low or no-charge accounts. Stay away from pointless ATM charges by utilizing your bank's ATMs or pulling out bigger amounts of cash less every now and again.

Budget-friendly entertainment: Look for free or cheap ways to entertain yourself in your community at places like parks, museums, community events, and festivals.

Bulk Purchase: In the long run, buying in bulk can help you save money on non-perishable goods. Simply ensure it's something you use routinely to stay away from squander.

Bill negotiations: Make sure of your bills, like web, link, or telephone administrations. By calling the service provider and asking for deals or discounts, you might get a better deal.

To Avoid Interest: Pay your bills on time whenever you can to avoid interest and late fees. Reduce your interest payments by paying off any loans or credit card debt you have as soon as possible.

Set Savings Objectives: Characterize clear reserve funds objectives, whether it's for an excursion, schooling, or a significant buy. You'll stay motivated to save if you set specific goals.

Keep in mind that saving money takes time and that it's alright to start small. Over time, you'll be able to achieve financial success if you stick to your financial goals and develop good money habits.

CHAPTER FOUR

Visa Requirement in Kosovo

However, keep in mind that visa policies can change, so official sources or the nearest Kosovo diplomatic mission or consulate should be consulted to confirm the current requirements.

Unrestricted entry: Residents of a few nations can enter Kosovo without a visa for short stays. This includes citizens of numerous nations, including the United States, Canada, Australia, the Schengen Area, and the European Union (EU). The span of allowed stay night shifts between 90 days inside a 180-day time frame or different circumstances in light of respective arrangements.

Visa-on-arrival: A visa can be obtained upon arrival at the Pristina International Airport for some nationalities that are not exempt from visa requirements. This visa usually only allows for a brief stay and has particular requirements and costs. However, prior to traveling, it is always preferable to determine whether this option is available for your nationality.

Visa application ahead of time: Before traveling, citizens of nations that are not eligible for visa-free entry or visa-on-arrival must apply for a visa at the closest Kosovo diplomatic mission or consulate. A valid passport, a visa application form, passport-sized photos, a travel itinerary, proof of sufficient funds, hotel reservations, and a letter of invitation are all possible requirements for obtaining a visa.

Permit for Temporary Residence: A Temporary Residence Permit (TRP) from the Ministry of Internal Affairs may be required if you intend to stay longer in Kosovo. The prerequisites for a TRP generally include giving motivations to your visit, confirmation of monetary means, medical coverage, and a spotless crook record.

Please keep in mind that these are only general guidelines; your nationality and the purpose of your visit may alter the specific requirements for a visa. Consult official sources like the Kosovo Ministry of Foreign Affairs or the closest Kosovo diplomatic mission or consulate for the most up-to-date and accurate information.

Tips for General Safety in Kosovo:

Know about your environmental elements: Always maintain vigilance and pay attention to the people and surroundings around you, whether you're exploring the outdoors or in urban areas.

Respect the traditions and customs of the area: Kosovo is a nation with distinctive customs and a rich cultural heritage. Dress modestly and with respect for the culture, especially when going to religious sites.

Utilize licensed taxis: To ensure your safety while traveling, choose licensed taxis or reputable ride-sharing services if you require transportation.

Secure your possessions: Keep your valuables, such as passports, cash, and electronics, safe and be cautious when you are in crowded areas to prevent petty theft.

Keep up with current happenings: Keep up to date on the country's political and security situation both before and during your trip. Keep an eye out for travel warnings issued by your government.

Avoid large-scale gatherings and political demonstrations: Although Kosovo is generally peaceful, political demonstrations and crowded gatherings should be avoided because of their potential for unpredictability.

Use ATMs in secure areas: To avoid card skimming or theft, use ATMs in reputable banks or in well-lit areas when withdrawing money.

Remain in legitimate facilities: Pick facilities with positive surveys and great safety efforts to guarantee a protected and agreeable stay.

Drink responsibly: Be responsible when you consume alcohol and be aware of your surroundings, especially in unfamiliar settings.

Learn essential neighborhood phrases: Really get to know a few fundamental neighborhood phrases, as it can assist in speaking with local people and can make your experience more pleasant.

Respect traffic laws: Be careful and obey traffic laws if you plan to drive or walk on the streets because traffic conditions can be unpredictable.

Keep crisis numbers helpful: Keep a list of local emergency numbers, such as those for the police, medical services, and embassy or consulate of your nation.

Keep in mind that although Kosovo is generally safe for tourists, you should always use common sense, be cautious, and put your safety first throughout your trip.

Kosovo Health consideration:

It is essential to consult local healthcare professionals and official health authorities in Kosovo for the most accurate and up-to-date health advice. Here are some broad **wellbeing contemplation:**

Facilities for healthcare: Although Kosovo's healthcare infrastructure has improved, it may not be as advanced as some developed nations. Facilities in major citieLiberiaiÅ¡tinana and Prizren are better equipped, but access to healthcare services may be limited in rural areas.

Vaccinations: Before traveling to Kosovo, make sure that all of your routine vaccinations, as well as any vaccinations that are recommended or required for travel, are current. Specific recommendations may be provided by your healthcare provider.

Food and water safety: To avoid water-borne illnesses, it is generally recommended to drink boiled or bottled water. Be careful while devouring food from road merchants and guarantee products of the soil are completely washed or stripped.

Sun Screening: Kosovo encounters a mainland environment, and UV radiation can be extraordinary, particularly in the late spring. Keep hydrated, apply sunscreen, and don protective clothing to avoid heat-related illnesses.

Diseases borne by ticks: Ticks may spread diseases like Lyme disease and tick-borne encephalitis in rural areas. Utilizing insect repellents and wearing protective clothing are preventative measures to take if you plan outdoor activities in grassy or wooded areas.

Voyager's The runs: In Kosovo, travelers may be at risk for diarrhea. Keep your hands clean, don't drink tap water, and be careful with raw or undercooked food.

Health Insurance: Guarantee you have thorough travel clinical protection that covers any possible health related crises, including clinical departure if necessary.

Prescriptions and Medication: Along with a copy of the prescription, bring a sufficient supply of any necessary prescription medications. In Kosovo, there may not be easy access to certain medications.

Polluting the Air: Air pollution can be particularly bad in Kosovo's major cities during the winter months. Extra precautions may be required for those with respiratory conditions.

Infectious Diseases: Be aware of any potential outbreaks of communicable diseases in the area and keep an eye on health advisories.

Keep in mind that the information presented here is not comprehensive, and specific travel and health advice for Kosovo should be obtained from official sources and healthcare professionals. When you travel, always put your health and well-being first.

Kosovo Currency:

There is no official currency for Kosovo. Kosovo uses the euro (€) as its official currency. This means that prices and transactions are paid in euros and Kosovo uses eurozone banknotes and coins rather than its own.

Please keep in mind that information about currencies can change over time, so it's best to check with current sources to make sure it's accurate.

Safety And Security in Kosovo:

It is essential to keep in mind that circumstances can alter over time, and for the most up-to-date information, it is best to look to more recent and up-to-date sources. I am able to provide some general information regarding security and safety measures that were applicable prior to my most recent update:

Situation in politics: Kosovo pronounced freedom from Serbia in 2008, yet the circumstance concerning its status stays a disputed matter. Kosovo and Serbia engaged in ongoing dialogue and negotiations to resolve unresolved issues.

Crime: Although petty theft and pickpocketing can occur in crowded areas or tourist destinations, Kosovo generally has a low crime rate. It is essential to exercise caution and keep an eye on your belongings, as with any destination where you travel.

Travel Warnings: Before going to Kosovo, it's always a good idea to check your government's travel warnings. These warnings give exceptional data on wellbeing and security worries, alongside any likely dangers or precautionary measures for explorers.

Protests: In Kosovo, demonstrations and protests can occur, typically in response to social or political issues. Although the majority of protests are peaceful, it is best to avoid large gatherings and keep an eye on local news for any developments.

Landmines: Landmines from previous conflicts may still be present in some parts of Kosovo. It is essential to stay on marked roads and paths when traveling in rural or off-the-beaten-path areas.

Traditions and Laws: Before going to Kosovo, learn about the local laws and traditions. Regarding the neighborhood culture and customs to stay away from any accidental offense.

Border regions: Due to historical and political considerations, some border regions near Kosovo may be sensitive. Avoid wandering into disputed territory and exercise caution.

As the circumstance can change after some time, I suggest checking with the most recent authority, government tourism warnings and other solid hotspots for any reports on wellbeing and security in Kosovo prior to arranging your visit.

Emergency Contact In Kosovo:

The emergency number in Kosovo is 112. Any kind of emergency, including police, fire, and medical situations, can be handled by dialing this number. The operator will connect you to the appropriate emergency service based on your situation when you call 112. When calling this number, it is essential to provide information about the emergency and your location that is both clear and concise. Please keep in mind that the emergency number 112 is used by everyone in the European Union, including Kosovo. It is intended to be not difficult to recall and open from any portable or fixed-line telephone. Do not hesitate to call 112 if you require immediate assistance in any EU country or Kosovo.

CHAPTER FIVE

Food And Drinks In Kosovo:

Kosovo's culinary heritage is diverse and extensive, having been influenced by a variety of cultures and traditions. It is situated in the center of the Balkans. Customary Kosovo cooking frequently includes good and delightful dishes that mirror the nation's set of experiences and geology. When you visit Kosovo, you can try the following well-known dishes and drinks:

Food FIFAlija: A remarkable and tedious dish, Flija is a layered baked good made with dainty crepe-like layers, substituting with different fillings like meat, cheddar, and yogurt. Cooking it typically takes several hours and is typically reserved for QebapaQebapa: Little, barbecued frankfurters produced using minced meat (normally a mix of sheep and hamburger) prepared with garlic and flavors. They are a common fast-food option that come with onions and bread.

: It's a flaky pastry that can be filled with meat, cheese, spinach, or pumpkin. It's also called burek. Pite is a popular snack that can be found in bakeries all over Kosovo.

Tavë Kosi: a delectable dish made of lamb or mutton and baked with eggs, yogurt, and spices. Rice and frequently a salad are often paired with this flavorful and creamy dish.

Flia: Flia is another type of layered pastry made with thin layers of dough and meat cooked in an oven or fireplace. It's a well known decision during merry events and get-togethers.

I'll go to Arra: A tasty dish made with chicken or sheep cooked with pecans, bringing about a superb blend of surfaces and tastes.

Sarma: Rice, spices, and minced meat are stuffed into cabbage leaves before being slowly cooked until tender.

Tava and Preparation: Lamb and vegetables are cooked in a clay pot to make a flavorful and aromatic stew, which is a Prizren specialty drinks:

Raki: A customary cocktail, Raki is an unmistakable cognac produced using refined natural products, generally grapes or plums. It's a popular option for parties and toasts.

Boza: a thick, sweet beverage made from fermented millet, corn, or wheat. Boza is frequently enhanced with cinnamon and is well known throughout the cold weather months.

Coffee: In Kosovo, coffee has a significant cultural significance. Numerous cafes serve both Turkish-style coffee, which is black, strong, and served in small cups, and European-style coffee.

Sharbat: A non-alcoholic beverage made with fruit extracts, sugar, and water. Cherry, rose, and pomegranate are just a few of the flavors available in Sharbat.

: Ayran is a traditional yogurt-based drink made with yogurt, water, and salt. It tastes tangy and is refreshing.

To fully appreciate Kosovo's delicious and varied cuisine, make it a point to visit the city's cafes, bakeries, and restaurants.

Local Cuisine And Specialist:

Kosovo, a landlocked nation in Europe's Balkans, has a rich and diverse culinary history that is influenced by its history and location. Kosovo's cuisine draws from Ottoman, Serbian, Albanian, and Mediterranean traditions, reflecting the country's cultural fusion. The following are some of Kosovo's most well-known dishes and specialties:FIFA: The Kosovo Albanian dish known as flija is similar to a layered pastry. It is made by stacking thin batter layers on top of one another on a heated metal plate or sa (a dome-shaped clay baking lid). Butter, cream, or yogurt are common fillings that are spread between each layer. After that, the flaja is baked until it resembles a rich, multilayered pie. **KosovaBurkeekek**: In the Balkans, burek is a staple, and Kosovo is no exception. It is a delectable pastry made of thin dough layers filled with potatoes, cheese, spinach, or minced meat. In most cases, the layers are rolled up to form a spiral, and it is typically served hot from the oven.

Kosi Tavi: Tav Kosi is a well-known Albanian dish that has established itself as a Kosovo culinary icon. It is a rice and lamb meat casserole that is baked, flavored with yogurt, eggs, and herbs like oregano. It is a delightful comfort food due to the combination of tender meat, creamy yogurt, and aromatic spices.

Gjakova Meat: Sausage dishes from Gjakova, a city in Kosovo, are well-known for their flavor. These sausages are made with minced meat, usually beef or lamb, and a mixture of spices like paprika, garlic, and black pepper. They are then air-dried or smoked, giving them their unmistakable taste.

Greek Salad: A basic yet scrumptious serving of mixed greens ordinarily found in Kosovo comprises new and fresh vegetables like tomatoes, cucumbers, onions, and chime peppers. It is frequently seasoned with salt, pepper, olive oil, and vinegar to produce a refreshing side dish that can be served with a variety of meals.

Pite: In Kosovo, pite refers to a wide range of savory pies from which to choose. Spinach, cheese, leeks, or pumpkin can all be used to fill these pies, which are wrapped in dough in thin layers.

Flia: Despite its similar name, Flia is a different dish. It is a pastry made of layers of dough and a variety of fillings. It is usually baked in an oven and rolled into a spiral. It is a popular option for celebrations and family gatherings.

Rakija, a Kosovar: Rakija is a traditional Balkan fruit brandy that is very popular. In Kosovo, it's frequently produced using grapes or plums and is an image of friendliness. It's filled in as an aperitif or a digestif during get-togethers and exceptional events.

These are just a few of the delectable dishes and regional specialties available in Kosovo. The country's cuisine is a true reflection of its history, culture, and people's warm welcome. Thus, assuming you at any point have the potential chance to visit Kosovo, make a point to enjoy these luscious joys and experience the exceptional kinds of the district.

Best Restaurants And Bars In Kosovo:

Some notable establishments include Tiffany Restaurant (Pristina), which is famous for its delectable Kosovar and Mediterranean fare and provides excellent service.

Soma Book Station (Prizren) is a restaurant and bookshop of one kind that offers a welcoming setting where you can enjoy excellent food and literature.

Liburnia (Pristina): This popular spot serves authentic Kosovar cuisine, including traditional Balkan dishes.

Trosha (Prishtina): Trosha provides a memorable dining experience by focusing on locally sourced ingredients and modernizing traditional recipes.

Gagi Restaurant (Peja): Gagi Restaurant, which is in the charming town of Peja, is well-known for its grilled specialties and warm atmosphere.

Dit' e Nat' (Pristina): Dit' e Nat' is a cozy café with a lively atmosphere. It serves delicious coffee, pastries, and light meals, making it the ideal spot to unwind.

Fusion Bar & Restaurant (Prishtina) combines a variety of culinary influences to produce an exciting and varied menu, as the name suggests.

Oda (Prizren): Oda is a charming restaurant that serves up traditional Kosovar fare in an old Ottoman house.

Libraria (Pristina) - Another bookshop café cross breed, Libraria allows you to partake in your feast encompassed by books and a wonderful climate.

Irish Bar (Pristina): Irish Bar has live music, a wide selection of drinks, and a friendly atmosphere for those who prefer a more casual setting.

Keep in mind that the restaurant and bar scene can change quickly, and it's possible that new establishments have opened since my last update. As a result, when looking for the best places to eat and drink in Kosovo, it's always a good idea to look at local listings and recent reviews.

Traditional Drink In Kosovo:

"Rakia," also known as "raki" or "Rakija," is a strong fruit brandy that locals typically make at home. It is one of the traditional drinks in Kosovo. Rakia is an indispensable piece of Kosovo's social legacy and is often shared during get-togethers, festivities, and unique events. It has significant social and cultural significance and is comparable to drinks found in other Balkan nations.

To make rakia, individuals utilize different organic products, with plum (called "slivovitz") being the most well known decision. However, a variety of other fruits, including grapes, apples, pears, quince, and apricots, are also utilized. After the fruit is crushed and fermented, a strong, clear alcoholic beverage is made by distilling the resulting mash.

Rakia is typically consumed undiluted and in narrow, small glasses. As a gesture of hospitality, it is common practice to serve small snacks or appetizers alongside a shot of rakia. The drink is well-known for its potent flavor, which varies depending on the fruit used and the distillation method.

Drinking rakia is ingrained in the culture of Kosovo, and it is frequently accompanied by toasts to honor friendship, family, and health. It is essential to consume rakia responsibly and in moderation, as with any other alcoholic beverage.

Kosovo's Nightlife and Shopping:

Shopping in Kosovo:

Kosovo offers a dynamic shopping experience with a blend of current shopping centers, customary business sectors, and nearby stores. A portion of the famous shopping objections in Kosovo include:

Prishtina's Albi Mall: Albi Mall, one of Kosovo's largest shopping malls, has a wide selection of restaurants, entertainment, and international and local brands.

Gërmia Shopping center (Prishtina): One more current shopping complex with different stores, a film, and a food court, giving an open to shopping experience.

Kalabria's Lagja (Prishtina): A bustling street in Prishtina with a lot of shops selling clothes, shoes, and accessories. It's a great place to look into current fashion trends in the area.

Fantastic Store (Prishtina): A retail chain in the core of the capital, offering an expansive determination of items going from dress to family things.

Gjakova's Old Bazaar: This conventional market in Gjakova features nearby specialties, gifts, and customary items, making it an extraordinary spot to encounter Kosovo's social legacy.

Night Market (Prizren): The Night Market in Prizren's historic center is a one-of-a-kind shopping experience, especially in the summer when you can find local handicrafts and delicious street food.

Kosovo's nightlife:

In recent years, Kosovo's nightlife scene has grown to include trendy bars, clubs, live music venues, and traditional establishments. Particularly in the major cities of Prishtina, Prizren, and Peja, the nightlife is lively. Some highlights include:

Str. (Prishtina) Bill Clinton: The bars, clubs, and lounges that line this street in the capital draw tourists and locals alike. It is the hub of Prishtina's nightlife.

Prishtina's Soma Book Station: An interesting spot that consolidates a book shop, bistro, and a bar. It frequently has unrecorded music exhibitions and widespread developments, making a loosening up climate.

Dit' e Nat' (Prishtina): a lively bar with a wide selection of drinks and cocktails during the day and a popular café at night.

Prishtina's ODA Theatre: A venue as well as a social place that habitually has shows, gatherings, and workmanship occasions, giving an elective nightlife experience.

Prizren's Te Rada: In Prizren, this bar offers a picturesque setting for drinks and socializing with friends near the river.

Peja Brew City (Peja): Peja Beer City is a must-see for beer enthusiasts. This brewery frequently hosts events that feature DJ sets and live music in addition to serving craft beers made in the area.

Peja's Rugova Canyon: Rugova Canyon is popular with locals and tourists alike during the summer for its late-night bonfires, music, and natural beauty.

Note: While enjoying the nightlife in Kosovo, it's important to be aware of your surroundings and to drink responsibly, just like in any other country. When planning your trip, it's always a good idea to check for the most recent recommendations and locations because nightlife and shopping scenes can change quickly.

CHAPTER SIX

Custom And TraditionIn Kosovo:

Certainly! Kosovo's rich cultural heritage is shaped by its history, diverse communities, and location in the Balkans. Let's take a look at some of Kosovo's traditions and **customs**:

Hospitality: Kosovars are known for their warm accommodation. Guests are treated with kindness and respect. It is common practice to bring a small token of appreciation when paying a visit.

Family Principles: Family holds a focal spot in Kosovo's way of life. Family ties are strong because extended families frequently live together or in close proximity to one another. The entire family participates in major life events like weddings and religious ceremonies.

Weddings: Numerous days are required for Kosovar weddings, which are elaborate and joyful affairs. Traditional music, dance, and vibrant attire distinguish them. During the wedding festivities, two or three families meet up to exhibit their social legacy.

Religion: Islam is practiced by the majority of people in Kosovo, with a significant Christian minority. Strict celebrations, like Eid al-Fitr (celebrated after Ramadan) and Christmas, are seen with enthusiasm and include local meetings and exceptional petitions.

Cuisine: The cuisine of Kosovo is influenced by the Balkans and the Ottoman Empire. "flija," a layered pastry, "burek," a savory pastry filled with meat or cheese, and "qebapa," grilled minced meat served with onions and bread, are popular traditional dishes.

Dance and Music: Kosovo's cultural expression is significantly influenced by traditional dance and music. Old stories, celebrations and exhibitions are held all through the country, displaying the dynamic and different customs of people.

Celebrations and Festivities: Numerous cultural festivals that honor Kosovo's heritage are held there. The "Dokufest," an annual international festival for short films and documentaries, is one such event.

Art and Carpets: Crafts and hand-woven carpets are an important part of Kosovo's cultural identity. Carpet weaving is a family tradition in many families, and these intricate patterns are frequently handed down through the generations.

Language and Personality: Albanian and Serbian are Kosovo's official languages. Both languages contribute significantly to the development of the nation's heritage, making language an essential component of cultural identity.

Tolerance toward religion: In spite of verifiable struggles, Kosovo has a practice of strict resilience and concurrence. It fosters a sense of unity when people from different religious backgrounds attend each other's religious ceremonies.

Due to the fact that Kosovo is home to a variety of ethnic and religious groups, it is essential to keep in mind that different communities' customs and traditions may differ. Some of the broad strands of Kosovo's cultural fabric can be seen in the aforementioned customs and traditions.

Language In Kosovo:

Kosovo has two official languages, making it a multilingual nation: Serbian and Albanian. The locals' day-to-day lives are significantly influenced by both languages. Allow me to furnish you with some data about every language:

Albanian:

In Kosovo, Albanian is the most spoken language. It belongs to the Albanian branch of the Indo-European language family. Most of Kosovo's populace, which is fundamentally made out of Albanians, involves Albanian as their local language. In educational, media, and government institutions, it is the primaLangleygua Serbianrbian:

The Serbian minority in Kosovo speaks Serbian, which is Kosovo's second official language. It is written in both Cyrillic and Latin scripts and is a South Slavic language. In areas where Serbs are the majority or a significant community, official documents, as well as schools, are written in Serbian.

Aside from Albanian and Serbian, a few different dialects are spoken in Kosovo because of its different populace and history. A portion of the minority dialects incorporate Bosnian, Turkish, Gorani, and Romani.

Because language plays a crucial role in shaping the cultural and social fabric of Kosovo, it is essential to comprehend and respect the country's linguistic diversity. Correspondence and understanding among various etymological networks are fundamental for encouraging harmony and collaboration in the district.

Music And Dance:

Kosovo's music:

Kosovo has a rich and different melodic legacy, impacted by its set of experiences, culture, and customs. Kosovo's traditional music is characterized by a combination of Balkan, Ottoman, and Albanian elements. "Iso-Polyphony," a distinctive form of polyphonic singing on the UNESCO list of endangered intangible cultural heritage, is one of Kosovo's most prominent forms of traditional music.

Notwithstanding customary music, current music genres like pop, rock, hip-jump, and electronic dance music have acquired prevalence in Kosovo, particularly among the more youthful ages. Kosovo's vibrant music scene has been bolstered by the appearance on the international stage of numerous talented bands and musicians.

Kosovo's dance:

Customary society moves assume a huge part in the social character of Kosovo. People moves are frequently performed at weddings, strict festivals, and other parties. These dances include

Roma, Albanian, Serbian, Turkish, and other cultural influences from the region.

The "Valle," or circle dance, is one of Kosovo's well-known traditional dances. It involves forming a circle with a group of people holding hands or linking arms and moving in unison to the beat of the music. Drums and traditional instruments like the "çifteli," a stringed instrument, frequently accompany the dance.

Hip-hop, breakdance, and other contemporary dance forms have gained popularity among young people in urban settings, particularly Pristina, the capital, and other major towns. In order to nurture and promote emerging talent in these contemporary dance styles, dance schools and workshops have emerged.

The dynamic and diverse nature of Kosovo's culture and people is reflected in the music and dance scene's ongoing development. Human expressions assume a critical part in communicating the nation's personality and associating its past with its present and future.

Arts And Craft In Kosovo:

Arts and crafts that reflect the region's history, traditions, and influences from various civilizations are part of Kosovo's rich cultural heritage. Some of the arts and crafts that are done in Kosovo are as follows:

Traditional Stitching: Embroidery is an important part of Kosovo's cultural heritage and has been around for a long time. Fabrics are sewed with intricate patterns and motifs, frequently using bright colors and geometric patterns. On decorative items, household goods, and clothing, traditional embroidery is common.

Weaving Rugs: Rug weaving is a strong tradition in Kosovo, resulting in exquisitely woven kilims and carpets. Rug weaving is usually a family or community activity with floral patterns, geometric shapes, and traditional symbols in the designs.

Woodcarving: Another traditional craft practiced in Kosovo is woodcarving, in which skilled artisans create intricate designs on furniture, doors, and other wooden items.

Decorative Jewelry: In Kosovo, filigree jewelry is a common form of handicraft. It involves creating fine jewelry pieces like earrings, necklaces, bracelets, and rings through intricate metalwork using delicate gold or silver threads.

Copper and Metal Craftsmanship: Beautiful copper and brass items, such as decorative plates, bowls, coffee sets, and traditional "Dezve" coffee pots, are made by skilled metalworkers in Kosovo.

Pottery and pottery: Pottery making in Kosovo has been around for centuries. Craftsmans make different stoneware things, including dishes, bowls, jars, and customary water containers called "Qarshia." Unique regional motifs and patterns are frequently incorporated into the designs.

Traditional instruments for music: Kosovo has a rich melodic legacy, and craftsmans make conventional instruments like the "lahuta" (a bowed instrument), "sharkia" (woodwind), and "çifteli" (a little, two-stringed lute).

Art and Icons of Religion: Kosovo has a past filled with delivering strict craftsmanship, especially Universal Christian symbols. These religious images are created by skilled painters using traditional techniques and styles.

Felt-making: The ancient art of felt-making is still practiced in some parts of Kosovo. Clothing, hats, and other decorative items can all be made from felted wool.

Traditional wear: An essential component of Kosovo's cultural heritage is the production of traditional costumes. These costumes often have distinctive embroidery, colors, and accessories that are specific to the region and the occasion.

Religion And Belief In Kosovo:

Religion and faith in Kosovo are different because of its verifiable and social foundation. Most of the populace rehearses Islam, with Sunni Muslims being the biggest strict local area. Moreover, there is a critical Christian

Conventional people group, particularly in the districts of North Kosovo and territories all through the country. Catholicism is likewise trailed by a more modest level of the populace.

The history of Kosovo and the interactions between its various ethnic and religious groups have shaped its religious landscape. The country's important values are tolerance and respect for religious diversity, and the Constitution guarantees freedom of religion.

Kosovo has been a region where various religious traditions have coexisted throughout its history, contributing to the rich tapestry of its people's beliefs and practices.

CHAPTER SEVEN

Kosovo Travel Tips:

The following are some travel recommendations for Kosovo:

Requirements for a Visa: Before traveling to Kosovo, verify the requirements for a visa. You may require a visa or be eligible for visa-free entry depending on your nationality.

Currency: The Euro (EUR) is Kosovo's official currency. Since not all establishments may accept credit cards, make sure you have some cash on hand.

Language: Albanian is the authority language, and many individuals additionally communicate in English, particularly in metropolitan regions and places of interest.

Safety: Tourists generally consider Kosovo to be safe. However, as with any other location, it is essential to maintain vigilance and follow standard safety measures.

Traditions of the region: Respect the traditions and customs of the area. Kosovo is a moderate society, so dressing unassumingly in strict locales and moderate regions is suggested.

Transportation: Major cities like Pristina have access to public transportation. Another common mode of transportation is the taxi. Consider renting a car if you intend to explore more remote regions.

Accommodation: There are a variety of lodging options, including budget hostels and luxury hotels. Pre-book, especially during peak travel times.

Cuisine: Try not to pass up on the chance to attempt customary Kosovar dishes like burek, flija, and baklava. Kosovo offers a different and delightful culinary experience.

Must-See Locations: Take a trip to Pristina, the capital, to see its historic landmarks and lively atmosphere. The renowned Newborn Monument is a must-see. The historic city of Prizren and the UNESCO-listed Visoki Deani Monastery are two additional places that must be seen.

Regard for History: Know that Kosovo has an intricate history. Before you go, you should learn more about the history of the area and the conflict that erupted there between 1998 and 1999 to get a better understanding of the country. Keep in mind, these tips are a beginning stage for your movement arranging. Before going on a trip, you should always check official travel guides and advisories for the most recent information. Have fun on your trip to Kosovo!

DO's and Don't For Tourists in Kosovo:

The following are some guidelines for tourists visiting Kosovo

DO's:

Regarding the nearby traditions and customs: Respect for their customs and traditions is essential because Kosovars are proud of their cultural heritage. It will be appreciated to shake hands and show common decency to others.

Visit cultural and historical locations: The Newborn Monument, the Old Town of Prizren, and the Graanica Monastery are just a few of Kosovo's many interesting cultural landmarks. Try not to botch the potential chance to investigate these destinations.

Try some of the local food: Kosovo offers various tasty customary dishes like burek, flija, and conventional barbecued meats. Accept the local cuisine and try new flavors.

Talk to one another: People from Kosovo are hospitable and friendly. Taking part in discussions with local people can prompt fascinating experiences about their way of life and lifestyle.

When going to religious locations, dress modestly: In the event that you intend to visit mosques or other strict spots, it's aware to dress unassumingly, covering your shoulders and knees.

Learn a few fundamental Serbian or Albanian phrases: Making an effort to speak a few local phrases can help you connect with the locals and show respect for their language, even though English is widely spoken in tourist areas.

Don'ts:

Avoid political discussion: The political situation in Kosovo can be delicate and complicated. To avoid any unintentional misunderstandings as a visitor, it is best to refrain from engaging in political discussions.

Try not to photo individuals without authorization: Before taking photos of locals, always ask for permission, especially in more conservative or rural areas.

Try not to talk about the war: For many Kosovars, the conflict between 1998 and 1999 was a difficult time. It's best not to talk about the war unless the people in the area do so.

Try not to litter: Recognize the lovely scenes of Kosovo by appropriately discarding your garbage. Contribute to environmental sustainability and cleanliness for future visitors.

Avoid crossing religious or ethnic **lines**: Because of the diverse population of Kosovo, it is essential to be mindful of cultural sensitivity.

Respect ethnic and religious differences while avoiding offense.

Try not to drink regular water: Even though the quality of the water has improved over the past few years, tourists still feel safer drinking bottled water.

You can have a more enjoyable and respectful visit to Kosovo if you adhere to these dos and don'ts. Have a great trip!

Conclusion

Kosovo is a fascinating destination with a unique blend of cultures, stunning landscapes, and a long history. Consider the following when creating a Kosovo travel guide:

Safety: Although Kosovo is generally regarded as a safe destination for tourists, it is essential to remain vigilant and aware of your surroundings, particularly in the larger cities. Follow any travel warnings issued by your government and remain informed about local events.

Attractions: Kosovo offers a blend of verifiable, social, and regular attractions. The Ethnological Museum and the Kosovo Museum are two interesting museums in Pristina, the capital. The Sharr Mountains and Ottoman-era architecture are highlights of the historic city of Prizren. Other eminent spots incorporate the Gracanica Religious community, Rugova Ravine, and the old city of Ulpiana.

Diverse Cultures: Kosovo is a blend of different societies, including Albanian, Serbian, and other ethnic networks. Respect the traditions of the area, appreciate the diversity, and interact with the welcoming locals.

Cuisine: The flavors of the Balkans and the Mediterranean are heavily present in Kosovo's cuisine. Traditional dishes like burek, sarma, and flia should not be missed. Drink rakija and local wines with your meals.

Accommodation: There are many places to stay in Kosovo, from expensive hotels to hostels and guesthouses that are affordable. It's best to reserve your lodging in advance, especially during peak travel times.

Transportation: Buses and trains are part of Kosovo's decent public transportation system, making it relatively simple to move around. Additionally, rental cars and taxis are available for additional flexibility.

Language: Albanian and Serbian are the official languages, but English is commonly spoken in tourist areas.

Local Happenings: To fully immerse yourself in Kosovo's authentic culture, look for local festivals, events, and cultural celebrations during your visit.

Check the most recent travel information including visa requirements, currency exchange rates, and any updated safety guidelines, prior to planning your trip. Additionally, if you want to plan a comprehensive and enjoyable trip to

Kosovo in 2023 and 2024, think about utilizing up-to-date travel guides, official tourism websites, and consulting a travel agency.

Printed in Great Britain
by Amazon

36264592R00066